On the Bus with
Joanna Cole

BY

Joanna Cole

WITH

Wendy Saul

CREATIVE · SPARKS

from HEINEMANN

On the Bus with

JOANNA COLE

· A CREATIVE AUTOBIOGRAPHY ·

HEINEMANN
Portsmouth, NH

Heinemann
A division of Reed Elsevier Inc.
361 Hanover Street
Portsmouth, NH 03801-3912

Offices and agents throughout the world

We would like to thank those who have given their permission
to include material in this book. Credits for borrowed
material appear on page 55.

Library of Congress Cataloging-in-Publication Data
Cole, Joanna.
On the bus with Joanna Cole/Joanna Cole, with Wendy Saul.
p. cm.—(Creative Sparks)
Summary: The author discusses her life, how she came to be a
writer, where she gets her ideas from, and what is
involved in producing a book.
ISBN 0-435-08131-4 (acid-free paper)
1. Cole, Joanna—Biography—Juvenile literature. 2. Women authors,
American—20th century—Biography—Juvenile literature.
3. Children's literature—Authorship—Juvenile literature. [1. Cole,
Joanna. 2. Authors, American 3. Women—Biography.
4. Authorship.] I. Saul, Wendy. II. Title. III. Series.
PS3553.04729Z465 1996
813'.54—dc20
[B] 95-40133 CIP AC

Editor: Carolyn Coman
Text and cover design: Virginia Evans, EvansDay Design
Manufacturing: Louise Richardson

Printed on acid-free paper.
99 98   RRD   4 5 6

Printed in Mexico.

To Phil and Rachel,

my loving family

A Thank-You Note

While it may take only one writer to create a manuscript, it takes many people to make a book. A writer like me, of picture books for children, is especially indebted to editors, art directors, and, of course, illustrators. In my career I have been fortunate to work with the finest in all these fields. Editors have encouraged, helped, and inspired me—people like Connie Epstein, David Reuther, Jane O'Connor, Craig Walker, Phoebe Yeh, Barbara Fenton, Barbara Greenman, and Norma Jean Sawicki. Art directors like Claire Counihan, Barbara Fitzsimmons, Ellen Friedman, Ronnie Herman, and Diana Klemin have chosen wonderful illustrators for my books and have cheerfully endured my habit of always putting in my two cents. Illustrators and photographers have given their all to make the books beautiful and informative; to mention only a few: Margaret Miller; Jerome Wexler; Maxie Chambliss; Alan Tiegreen; Dirk Zimmer; Aliki; Jared Lee; M. K. Brown; Lynn Munsinger; and, of course, Bruce Degen, my friend and the illustrator of the *Magic School Bus* series. Finally, I owe a great deal to my friend and colleague Stephanie Calmenson. For many years we have worked together on anthologies and fiction, and we have been our own writers group of two, reading and commenting on each other's work. I know my books are much better for her wise counsel. To all these talented and dedicated people, and to others too many to name, go my heartfelt admiration and thanks.

Contents

ONE

Did You Know That...?

WHY I WRITE WHAT I WRITE

My father was a very intelligent man who could do just about anything, but he didn't think of himself as intelligent. That's because he had dyslexia and never could read very well as a child. In those days, people didn't know about dyslexia, and his teachers punished and shamed him for it. Later in life he taught himself to read the newspaper, but he never became a real reader.

One day, when I was about twelve or thirteen, I was lying on the sofa immersed in a novel. My father came by and asked with genuine curiosity, "What is it like to read a book like that?" I told him about the experience of reading—about how the words on the page seem to disappear and you become lost in the story, seeing pictures and hearing voices in your head. I felt a new appreciation of an intense pleasure that I had simply taken for granted before and sorry that my father could not share it.

You might think that a man who did not read or write very much could not be a strong influence on a writer. But that isn't true at all of my father and me. He was a fabulous storyteller. He entertained the family with stories about his life as a boy and young man. And, at the dinner table, he argued vehemently with us about everything under the sun—from presidents to religion to racism. As a result, he was not the easiest

My family in about 1950. From left to right are: me; my sister, Virginia; my mother; and my father.

person to live with (or to eat with), but he gave me a sense of argument—of how one idea follows another, how things are supposed to make sense.

My father also showed me, by his own example, how to work. He had a housepainting business when I was growing up, and left the house at six in the morning and came back after five in the afternoon six days a week. After dinner, he often went to the basement and mixed paints from pigment, lead, and oil. (In those days, they didn't have good ready-made paints.) Sometimes I would follow him downstairs and talk with him while he mixed. He always told me how important it was to do good work no matter how small a job might be.

In school, I followed my father's example. I

worked hard (which was good), and I argued (which sometimes caused problems). I was passionate about ideas. If I thought something was wrong or didn't make sense, I had no qualms about disagreeing with other students and teachers. Once I even made a junior high school teacher cry. (I still feel sorry about that.)

Whenever I had a writing assignment, I attacked it with relish. I loved making one idea follow another. I loved making sense of things. If I had to do a report on honeybees or the La Brea Tar Pits or Benjamin Franklin, it never occurred to me just to copy down one fact after another. My mind naturally made a story-argument out of the subject. Later when I began writing children's books, I did the same thing. I have never written a book about a subject that did not interest me. In that way, I hope my books will interest my readers, too.

Since I loved to write when I was a child, you might think that I always knew I would be a writer by profession. But I didn't, because I didn't know any writers,

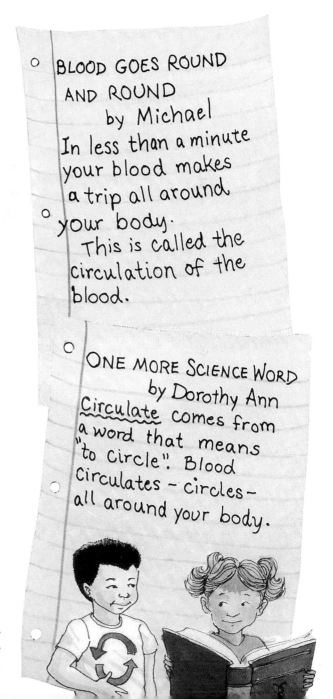

I loved to write school reports when I was a kid, and I still write them for the Magic School Bus *books. Illustration by Bruce Degen from* The Magic School Bus Inside the Human Body.

and I didn't know that a housepainter's daughter could become a writer. As I grew up, I had many other jobs. In East Orange, New Jersey, where I lived, I babysat, I worked in the library, I washed out test tubes at the Department of Health laboratory. Later I worked on an assembly line making television sets, and after I moved to New York City, I was a teacher and a librarian, I answered letters for a news magazine, I became a proofreader for a while, and finally I was an editor of children's books. These jobs showed me that I could be a writer, too.

Illustrations by Jean Zallinger from my first science book, Cockroaches, *published in 1971.*

Since my favorite subject in grade school had been science, and since I had been an avid watcher of insects as a child, I decided to write a children's book about insects. But all the insects I thought of had already been done. My father told me about an article he had read in the newspaper about cockroaches, and how they were "living fossils," animals that hadn't changed much since prehistoric times. This interested me, so I wrote a book about cockroaches. Imagine how lucky I was that an editor liked my manuscript and published it—even though it was about a subject that almost everyone finds disgusting and horrible!

Once I saw that I could write and be published, I started thinking about other things to write about. I wrote many science books—a book about how a puppy is born, one about cars and how they go, a series about animals' bodies, one about evolution. I also wrote funny storybooks—a series about a family of clowns called the *Clown-Arounds,* a story about a witch called *Bony-Legs,* a series about two monster best friends named Rosie and Prunella.

One of Jared Lee's funny illustrations for Monster Manners.

But I always thought of myself first and foremost as a science writer. People have asked me, "Are you a scientist?" and "Did you study science in school?" The answer is no to the first question and yes to the second. But more important than what I studied in school were the books and magazine and newspaper articles I read outside school. When I went to college, I liked my classes, but I was more excited about the college bookstore. In class I might be reading a botany book or a Spanish text—but in the bookstore I found a book called *The Badger* by an Englishman who had spent years camping out in the woods, watching these furry animals as they came out of their underground tunnels. A while ago, my mother found a letter I'd written to her from college. In it I said, "Did you know that…" and listed five or six fascinating tidbits I'd found out from my bookstore reading. Amazingly, it turned out that over the years I'd written children's books about almost every one!

TWO

Jumping Beans, Magic Buses, & One Weird Science Teacher

GETTING A GOOD IDEA

Illustration by Lynn Munsinger from
Norma Jean, Jumping Bean.

One day, when I had been an author for about fifteen years, I was walking down the street thinking about one of my editors, whose name is Norma Jean Sawicki. Suddenly the phrase *Norma Jean, Jumping Bean* sprang into my mind. I immediately realized that this would be a terrific title for a book about a little girl kangaroo, and when I got home I started writing it. By the way, Norma Jean, the editor, is *not* jumpy and she doesn't even know that her name was the inspiration for that book!

Many of the fiction stories I've written come from folktales I love. For instance, *Bony-Legs* and *Doctor Change* are retellings of folktales; *Monster Manners* is about me and my childhood best friend; and the plots for the *Clown-Arounds* came from experiences I've had with my family—such as the year we all had the flu at the same time.

When I write nonfiction, I often choose subjects I've always been curious about: evolution, how cuts and bruises heal, how a chick grows inside an egg. At other times, editors may suggest topics: how spiders catch food, how our senses work, even how *I* work—the book you're reading now.

Occasionally, I get an idea for a new book from one I wrote before. For example, in 1977, when I was working on *A Fish Hatches,* I was fascinated to learn how a fish is adapted for swimming and breathing underwater. This gave me the idea for a series about animals' bodies. The first book was *A Frog's Body,* about how an air-breathing animal can be perfectly suited to live in water. We can easily see how a frog's webbed feet make it a good swimmer. But even features that don't seem important often have a use. A frog's funny stick-up eyes mean the frog can stay *under* the water while still keeping a look out *above* the water for insects to eat.

Photograph by Jerome Wexler from A Frog's Body.

Sometimes a book comes out of a very personal experience I've had. I wrote *How You Were Born* for our daughter, Rachel, when she was four years old. Later, when my husband and I tried to adopt a child, we met many adoptive parents

Photograph, left, by Margaret Miller from How You Were Born, *and illustration, below, by Maxie Chambliss from* How I Was Adopted: Samantha's Story.

and children. We finally ended up not adopting, but over and over, I heard the words, "You should write a book about adoption like the one you wrote about birth." Eventually I did: *How I Was Adopted: Samantha's Story.*

It's just a coincidence that the two pictures are so similar— even down to Dad's striped shirt!

The basic idea for the *Magic School Bus* books came from an editor at Scholastic, Craig Walker. Craig was a big fan of the *Clown-Around* books. He was also the editor of the See-Saw Book Club at Scholastic. He was looking for a way to get kids more interested in science books, and he had the

The Clown-Arounds were
in an awful pickle.
Everyone was in bed—even the doctor!
There was only one thing to do.

Bubbles quickly wrote a note
and gave it to Wag-Around to deliver.

A double-page spread from Get Well, Clown-Arounds, *with pictures by Jerry Smath.*

idea of a humorous book about a teacher who takes her class on magical field trips to learn about science. But he didn't have anyone to write the book. One day, Craig realized that the *Clown-Arounds* author was the same author who had written so many serious science books—me. He picked up the phone and dialed my number.

I was enchanted with the idea. I thought it would be so much fun to write. Craig and I met and tossed around ideas for exciting places the class might visit: the moon; the Egyptian pyramids; prehistoric times. Craig also mentioned that they might visit the town waterworks. This he thought was *not* such an exciting place. But I loved it because I imagined that the teacher would be enthusiastic about the trip, while the children would think, "How boring!" I thought this combination would make the book funny, and I knew that it could be successful only if the science was rock solid and the plot was exciting and humorous.

One of my tasks in coming up with the *Magic School Bus* books was to develop the

*Illustrations of
Ms. Frizzle by
Bruce Degen.*

teacher's character. Craig had talked about his teachers, and, as I created Ms. Frizzle, I found myself remembering mine from elementary and junior high school. Did I have a teacher like Ms. Frizzle? Yes and no. None of my science teachers in East Orange had magical powers on field trips, but they were the best.

One teacher, Miss Bair, was my favorite. Like Ms. Frizzle, she was very serious about science. She did not try to "make it interesting to kids," she just communicated her own interest to us. Like Ms. Frizzle, she just barged ahead doing an experiment with Ping-Pong balls and a vacuum cleaner or manipulating a

model of an atom—so involved in what she was doing that she blithely ignored our reactions. My Ms. Frizzle does the same thing— pulling the kids along on the coattails of her own excitement in her subject. (The Ms. Frizzle in the books *acts* like Miss Bair, but *looks* like Bruce Degen's high school geometry teacher, Miss Isaacs. I'll tell more about Bruce later.)

As an adult, I remembered Miss Bair with affection and admiration. Imagine my surprise, then, when after having written several *Magic School Bus* books, I discovered my eighth-grade diary under a pile of sweaters

JANUARY 9

Dear Diary,

I did my project this morning in science. Miss Bair made Chris and I do it together. Did we have fun! Old lady Bair kept talking about the educational points of a microscope. All the kids kept saying how educated they were getting, and we were having hysterics.

I got all my corrections and make-up work done in Math and I am very happy.

Jo

and turned to an entry about science class. There was a most unflattering description of my favorite teacher. I called her "Old Lady Bair" and the comments from me and my classmates could have come straight out of the mouths of *Magic School Bus* kids. It was

then that I realized that the kids in my books may *say* that the Friz is weird, and they may groan when she announces a field trip, but in their hearts they love and admire her—even Arnold!

Whenever we think about ideas for *Magic School Bus* books ("we" being me, Bruce Degen, and the editors at Scholastic) we try to come up with "big" topics that kids, teachers, and parents are interested in and think are important. For instance, we did a book about ocean science, rather than a whole book about sharks or seaweed. We did the human body, not the mouth or the ear. We did the solar system, not a whole book about a single planet.

Usually when an idea comes—let's say it's the solar system—I already have a general idea of the structure of the book. I know right away that the bus will have to turn into a space ship so that the class will visit each planet. At first, I don't know what events will lead up to this. But pretty soon, ideas start forming. I picture the class in school, then I ask myself, how will they get started on the trip? And it occurs to me that they'll be going to the planetarium and get sidetracked into space. To make things a little different, I think of having Arnold's cousin, Janet, visit the class. All this goes into a two-page essay/outline that I send off to my editor. As I keep thinking, researching, and eventually writing the story, I get ideas for the details: I figure out that the class can't go to the planetarium because it's closed that day and they have to go to outer space instead; I write word balloons for Janet and she turns into a know-it-all; and by the time the bus/space ship gets to the asteroid belt, I need a plot element to make things more exciting, so the Friz gets lost in space and the kids are left on their own.

At the same time that I am fleshing out the plot and giving the characters things to say, I am still reading, reading, reading about my subject. I want the science to be rock solid.

THREE

Don't Worry. We Have Plenty Back at the Lab.

INFORMATION—HOW TO FIND IT

In preparing to write a science book, I always read much more than one would think I needed to. I read as many books as I can find on the subject. I look in libraries and bookstores. I ask for help from librarians. I dip into the computer at the library. I try to find articles in scientific magazines, and I search for videos about my subject. Sometimes, but not always, I read children's books to see how other authors have handled the subject.

Basically, I'm a reader. If I have read two books and three articles on coral reefs, and then I watch a TV special about them, chances are I will already know almost everything on the show. I believe in reading!

As I read, I absorb an enormous amount of information. I take some notes, but I'm not very traditional. I don't keep files of carefully coded index cards, for instance. But that isn't to say I'm not well organized. Early in my reading, I abandon the rough outline I made previously and make a blank dummy out of typing paper. I number the pages and write some words in pencil on each page—for instance, in the *Dinosaur* dummy, one page was marked "In the classroom—it's visitors day" and another was "Time machine," another, "Dinosaur dig—which bones are which?" and still another,

Here are some "outtakes" from the Magic School Bus *book on honey bees. Some of these reports and word balloons never made it into the final book.*

"Sauropods—special stomach." Then as I read, I write down on sticky notes any special information I don't want to forget and attach the notes on the appropriate dummy pages.

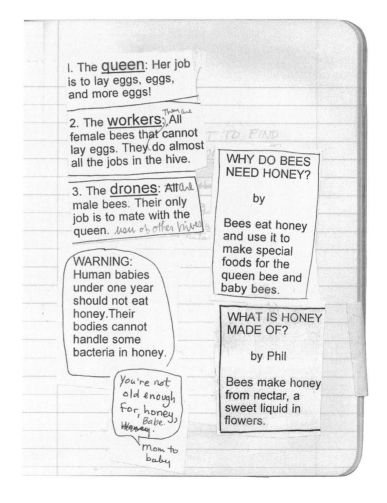

Later I begin to work on the computer, writing the actual book. For a *Magic School Bus* book, I write the text, the word balloons, and the school reports in different files. As I go along, I print them out, cut them up, and tape them into the dummy. Gradually, the blank dummy gets filled up and becomes a complete manuscript of the book. In the process, the original notes I made get covered up, so at the end of the writing, I can't really find them anymore.

Part of my research is finding an expert on my subject. For instance, in 1980, when I was writing *A Snake's Body,* I needed to talk to

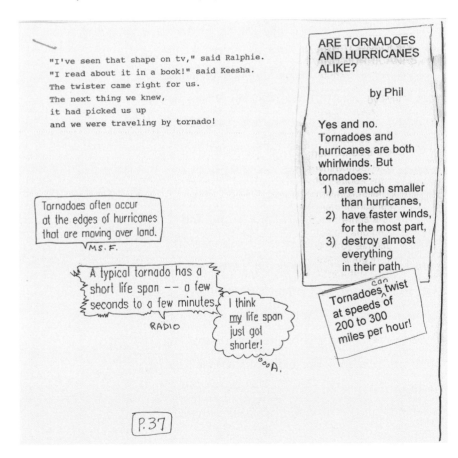

Here is a dummy page from The Magic School Bus Inside a Hurricane.

a snake scientist. I had some specific questions to ask, and I wanted someone to read what I had written and tell me if I'd got it right.

I lived in New York City, down the street from the Museum of Natural History. I called the museum and spoke to a friendly snake expert. "I live close by," I said. "I can come to see you at the museum." But the scientist felt like getting some fresh air, and he suggested that he walk over to my apartment. When he arrived, I showed him my dummy and asked him my questions, while Taffy, my Yorkshire terrier, slept on the floor next to my chair. Finally, the snake expert said, "The snakes in our lab shed their skins frequently, and I brought along a snakeskin just to show what they look like." He pulled out a transparent skin from his bag and reached over to give it to me. Instantly, Taffy's eyes sprang open, she leaped into the air, grabbed the skin with her teeth and ran into the bedroom, where she disappeared under the bed. Later she re-emerged, but the snakeskin was gone forever.

"Don't worry," said the scientist, "we have plenty of them back at the lab."

I know how much I owe the experts who help me and the scientists who find out all the interesting information I use in my writing. Without scientists, I as a writer would have nothing to report, and all of us as a culture would be significantly poorer. I know that I am not a scientist; I am a science writer, which is quite different. My job is to try to understand scientists' complex ideas and to communicate them in a way that makes sense to my readers.

Bruce Degen and I visited the hives of our friend Mark Richardson as part of our research on honey bees. A few seconds after Bruce took this picture of me and Mark, a bee flew up my trouser leg and panicked. It stung me and it hurt. I felt bad for the bee, because bees die soon after stinging.

FOUR

Why Are Leaves Green?

WRITING ABOUT THE HOWS AND WHYS

For a science writer, it doesn't matter what the topic is, as long as it interests you. Because science isn't about *what,* it's about *how* and *why.* Let's say that you are waiting for the school bus, and you notice the leaves on the trees around you. You remember you have a school report due soon. Maybe it could be about leaves.

How would I, Joanna, begin such a report? First, here's what I wouldn't do. I wouldn't decide right there at the bus stop what the report would say. I wouldn't go to the encyclopedia as soon as I got to school and start copying down information. I wouldn't make an outline. Some other writers might do these things successfully. But not me. First, I would read.

I would read in a very relaxing way. At the library, I would find encyclopedia articles on trees and on plants, and I'd see if there was a separate article on leaves. If possible, I would photocopy these and take them with me. I would ask the librarian to help me find a few good books on plants with chapters on leaves. If there were a whole book on leaves, all the better.

That evening, I would spread all the stuff on my bed. (Some other writers might put it on a desk or a table.) My little dog Muffy would sleep on one book, while I ate crackers and read. (I wouldn't let my three big dogs on the bed because they would crumple all the papers.) I wouldn't worry about reading every word. I would keep an open mind. I wouldn't want to pick out the first six facts that I found and write them down one after another without feeling a connection to my subject. I would want to see which information answered questions I've

always had about leaves. Sometimes these might be questions I didn't even know I had until I found the answers. For instance, why maple trees have big flat leaves and pine trees have skinny needles; why leaves are green; why they have veins.

I notice as I read that leaves are not there just to look pretty. In nature almost everything has a function, a reason for being that makes sense. Leaves have work to do. They are green because they have a green chemical called chlorophyll that is used to change light energy into food. Maple trees and other trees that are bare in winter have big, flat leaves with a large surface area to catch more sunlight to manufacture more food in the summer to make up for all those winter months when the tree doesn't have leaves. Evergreens usually have small, waxy-coated needles to conserve water during the long, dry winter, when water is often frozen and not available to plants. And because needles stay on in winter, evergreens can do some extra food-making on warm, sunny winter days, making up for what they miss on account of their small size. Leaves have veins that carry water up from the tree's roots because to make food, leaves need water, as well as chlorophyll, sunlight, and carbon dioxide from the air. Finally, an idea for my report starts taking shape. How about a report called "Leaves Are Food Makers"?

So now I will take notes about leaves as food makers. I won't worry about all the other facts about leaves. I will use facts to *explain* how leaves work to make food. So the report won't be just a stack of facts. It's sort of like a story, and it's sort of like an argument. It has a beginning, a middle, and an end, starting with the sun shining on the leaf and ending with the veins carrying the food away to other parts of the tree and water vapor and oxygen exiting the leaves through pores.

This is the way I wrote school reports when I was young, and this is the way I write my science books today, books like *Your Insides: The Human Body: How We Evolved* and *You Can't Smell a Flower With Your Ear.* Writing a Magic School Bus book is the same, but of course, it's a little different, too.

I Knew I Should Have Stayed Home Today!

WRITING THE *MAGIC SCHOOL BUS* BOOKS

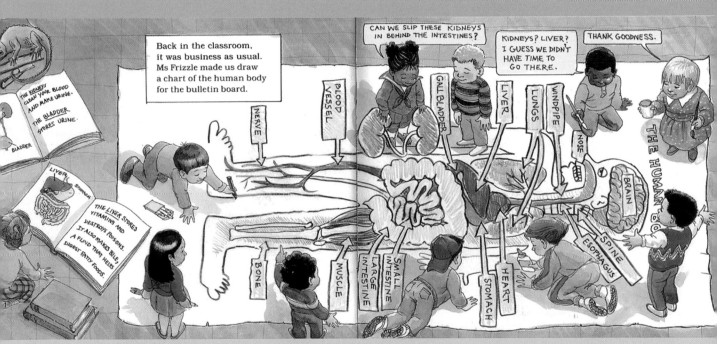

A double page with illustrations by Bruce Degen from The Magic School Bus Inside the Human Body.

In every *Magic School Bus* book, the science is the skeleton of the book. It forms a frame on which the fiction part of the book hangs. Everything I said about writing a report on leaves applies to writing the science in a *Magic School Bus* book. When I first started the book that became *The Magic School Bus Inside the Earth,* for example, I thought it was going to be about the inside of a volcano. But as I began reading about volcanoes, I realized that what was interesting about them for me was how the stuff that spews out of a volcano connects to the whole earth. So I ended up writing a book about what the earth is made of and how, even though it seems so solid and unchanging to us, it is really moving and transforming itself all the time. But I certainly didn't want to forget about such an exciting thing as a volcano. I knew right away that Ms. Frizzle's class trip would have to end with the bus being shot out of a volcano. What else?

A page from The Magic School Bus Inside the Earth

Red-hot lava came streaming out of the volcano.
Some of it shot into the air like a fountain.
Some of it flowed over the land like a river.
Our bus went along with it—right into the sea.

CLASS, WHEN THIS LAVA HARDENS, IT WILL BE THE NEWEST ROCK ON EARTH.

WHO CARES? JUST GET US OUT OF HERE!

HISSSSS

HISSSSS

HISSSSSSSS

Bruce Degen's pictures of Arnold.

I talked a little bit earlier about Ms. Frizzle's being like Miss Bair, but Ms. Frizzle is also like me. She likes to learn about science and she likes to explain it to her class, just as I like to explain it in my books.

You probably know Arnold, the kid who likes to stay home, who doesn't want to get too messy, too cold, or too involved in anything. The kid who would rather watch a filmstrip than be an astronaut. Arnold is like me, too. I spend most of my time reading and writing. I sometimes thank my lucky stars that I am not at this moment on an expedition to the North Pole. (Although, as my husband points out, I whine too much about the cold ever to be invited on such a trip.)

Arnold is the character I feel closest to in the books. He also is a character who evolved without my being aware of it. It happened when I was writing the first book, *The Magic School Bus at the Waterworks.* I had just written the text that makes the bus float

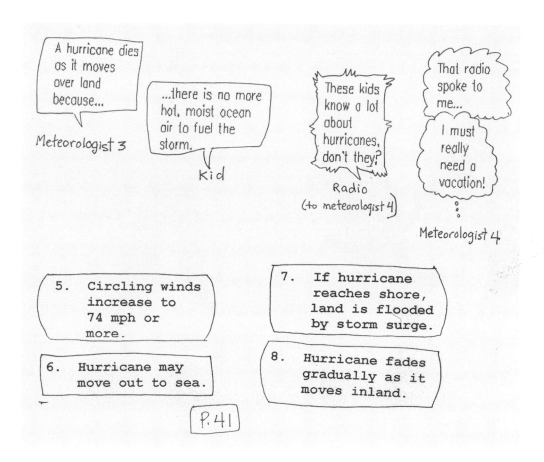

up into a cloud, and I started making up word balloons coming from inside the bus. One kid said, "We're going up!" Ms. Frizzle's balloon explained about evaporation, and because her explanation was a little bit long and maybe, I feared, a little bit boring, I had Ms. Frizzle add, "Arnold, are you paying at-

Here's what my dummy page looked like for page 41 in The Magic School Bus Inside a Hurricane . . .

and here's Bruce Degen's pencil sketch for the same page. Notice that I was still rewriting the word balloons at this stage.

tention?" At that point, Arnold wasn't a real person, he was just a name. But the next balloon that sprang to mind was Arnold's answer, a thought balloon saying, "I knew I should have stayed home today." On a previous page I had written a kid's balloon saying, "I want my mommy." Now I knew who had said it. And I had him say it again, because the class trip was getting scarier by the minute, so anyone who needs mom once, needs her twice.

And the very next time Arnold gets a balloon, it's when the class shrinks. Arnold's thought balloon says, "I was *already* small for my age." I had started to see Arnold in my mind as a real person.

When I was writing that first *Magic School Bus* book, I had a few problems to solve. The first was how to get all that science and story and humor into one picture book. I ended up creating a special format, or design, for the book, breaking up the text and putting some of it in a story, some in word balloons and some in school reports (my favorite form of writing, remember?). I also realized that for the children to go on trips where no kids have gone before, the bus must behave magically. So I had the bus take on the pattern on Ms. Frizzle's dress (an octopus print) as it passes under a bridge,

and begin floating into the air. Of course,
the bus became much more adventurous in
future books, turning into a space ship, a
time machine, a weather plane, even a surf-
board.

Everyone knows that the *Magic School Bus* books are full of jokes. There are puns, when one word is used in two different ways, and there are riddles, which actually are puns in disguise. But, for me, what really makes the books funny are the characters. In real life, it is most often a teacher who says: sit down, read a book, be quiet, finish your work. And it is the kids who say: let's get out of here, let's do something fun, let's run around. But in the books, the roles are reversed. It's the Friz who wants to get messy and the kids who wish they could just take spelling tests like other classes.

Some *Magic School Bus* situations are based on things that happened in my life. For instance, in *The Magic School Bus Inside the Earth,* the kids get an assignment to bring a rock to school. The next day, almost everyone has some excuse, and the kids who actually brought a rock have messed up in some way. Arnold, for one, has brought a piece of Styrofoam covered with dirt. This actually happened to my daughter, Rachel, when she was in second grade. We went rock

"Arnold, that looks like Styrofoam to me."

collecting in a park near our New York apartment. Rachel came running over to me, bubbling with excitement. "Mommy, Mommy, look at this *terrific* rock!" I looked and immediately realized that it was a piece of Styrofoam covered with dirt, but I didn't have the heart to tell her.

I often get letters from *Magic School Bus* readers saying "Your books are so funny" and "You must be funny, too." I really do write the jokes in the books, but if you were to meet me, I might not make you laugh. Most of my humor goes into my books.

Sometimes I can't tell whether something's going to be funny or not. Sometimes I write a word balloon and I say to myself, I'll rewrite that later. Then someone comes and reads it and laughs hysterically. Still later people may tell me, "That's the funniest thing in the book." For instance, in *The Magic School Bus Inside the Earth,* when the class first begins to study about the earth, there is a wall display titled "Challenge of the Week: Which One Is the Earth?" Under these words are pictures of an orange, an alphabet block, and the planet earth. When I first stuck that onto my dummy page, I thought it was a little lame. But my editor liked it, and later a book reviewer in *The New York Times* mentioned it as something she and her family had found especially funny.

Is Ms. Frizzle funny? She *seems* funny with her crazy dresses and shoes, but if you look closely you'll see that the Friz is really a straight man. She's the part of the comedy team who says something serious so that another comedian can make a joke of it. In *The Magic School Bus on the Ocean Floor,* the Friz says, "Most of the seafood we eat comes from here on the continental shelf, Arnold." And Arnold thinks, "I thought it came from the supermarket shelf."

Sometimes I write several jokes for the same space. In *The Magic School Bus in the*

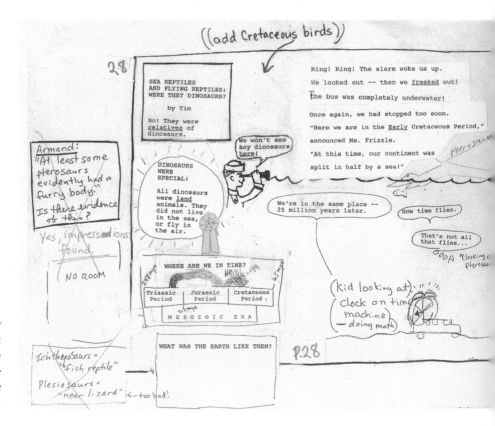

Here is my original dummy for pages 28 and 29 in The Magic School Bus in the Time of the Dinosaurs. *I wanted to include everything here and more, but there is never enough room.*

Time of the Dinosaurs, I had a whole bunch of jokes on the pages where the land is completely covered by an inland sea. Flying reptiles swoop down on the class from above, marine reptiles swim up and peer in the windows, and the school bus/time machine doesn't seem all that watertight, either. One kid says, "I hate to mention this, BUT…a time machine isn't a submarine!" Someone answers, "Hey, that rhymes," and another says, "Hey, this leaks." "I'm homesick," wails someone else, and Arnold thinks, "I'm seasick!" while Phoebe laments, "At my old school, the bus didn't leak." Finally, a practical kid requests, "Can't we find a drier time, Ms. Frizzle?" If you get a chance to look at the book, you can check and see which jokes made it to press.

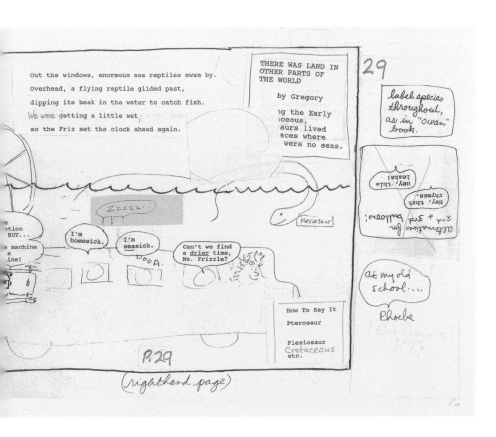

SIX

Bruce, Have You Painted Neptune Yet?

WORKING WITH OTHERS

Bruce and I, with our editor, Phoebe Yeh, working on a book together.

So far I have been talking as if I work all alone. For the most part that is true. I am usually sitting in front of a blank page trying to figure out what will go on it. But it takes many creative people to make a book.

The main people I work with are editors. An editor helps a writer by suggesting ideas, talking over problems, reading manuscripts and asking for revisions, and generally being on the writer's side in a difficult business. Different editors draw out different sides of me. For instance Craig Walker helped get the *Magic School Bus* series started. Jane O'Connor has encouraged me to write easy-to-read books such as *Hungry, Hungry Sharks* and *You Can't Smell a Flower With Your Ear.*

David Reuther inspires me to write very personal books about children and how they grow—books like *How You Were Born, The New Baby at Your House,* and *How I Was Adopted: Samantha's Story.*

Art directors are responsible for making a book look good. They decide who will illustrate a book, and then they do for the artist what the editor does for the writer. I know some of the artists and photographers who have worked on my books, but I have never even met most of them. We each work on the books independently through our editor and art director.

One artist I know well is Bruce Degen, the author-illustrator of *Jamberry,* among other books, and who illustrates the *Magic School Bus* books. Bruce and I had never met when we started the series, but because the books are so complicated, Craig Walker, who was then the editor, and Bruce and I had a

Bruce and some of his pencil sketches for the Dinosaur book. Turn back to pages 38–39 to see how much he improves my original dummy pages.

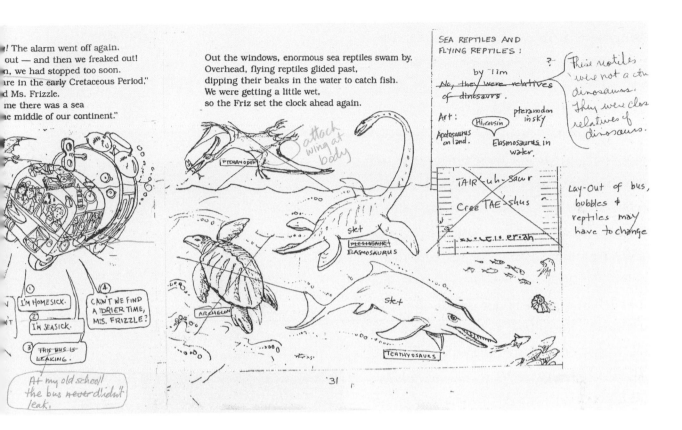

meeting about the first one. Bruce and I have become good friends since, and we and our families even live in the same town now.

How do Bruce and I work together? Except for revisions, I write the book first, and then Bruce illustrates it. After Phoebe Yeh, who is now the editor, and I and the scientific consultants have decided that my dummy is done, it goes to Bruce. He makes a sketch dummy and shows it to me and Phoebe and the scientific consultants. Once I see his sketches, Phoebe and I may decide that something written previously doesn't seem clear or funny, and I'll rewrite. Then

Bruce may have to revise his sketches. Finally, Bruce is able to begin doing the final paintings. Sometimes, however, we have to make more changes even then.

When we were working on the solar system book, the Voyager space probes were still traveling from planet to planet. One day, I called Bruce and asked, "Have you painted Neptune yet?" "Why do you ask?" Bruce said cautiously, because he suspects that I enjoy changing things right up to the last minute just to make his life difficult.

"You've got to look at Newsweek," I said excitedly. "They've got pictures of Neptune. There's a Great Dark Spot. They never knew it was there before!" Bruce looked at Newsweek and heaved a sigh of relief. He *had* painted Neptune already, but to create the Great Dark Spot, all he had to do was apply one smear of dark gray paint on the planet's blue surface.

I love to work with Bruce because he makes the *Magic School Bus* books what they are. He can draw *anything,* and he makes it funny and accurate. He modeled the kids in

The page showing Neptune from The Magic School Bus Lost in the Solar System.

the books after his own children's friends, working from class pictures. Bruce is a big bear of a guy (which may be why he paints so many bears in his books), and he's always making puns and jokes, so he's fun to be with. We often travel together to make author appearances at conferences and bookstores. While we're on the airplane, we talk about the books. Back home, Bruce and his wife, Chris, and I and my husband, Phil, often get together for dinner and conversation.

Bruce and I autographing in a bookstore.

Do Bruce and I compete with each other? We sure do. I say the words are most important in our books, and he says the pictures are. We'll probably never agree on this issue, but on almost everything else, we're a very compatible team.

Sometimes I collaborate with other writers. I often work with my friend Stephanie Calmenson, the author of well-known picture books like *The Principal's New Clothes, Dinner at the Panda Palace* and *Rosie, A Visiting Dog's Story.* Stephanie and I met when we were both working as editors in the children's book department at Doubleday, and over the years, we have created quite a few

Stephanie Calmenson and Rosie.

books together including: *Crazy Eights,* a book of card games; *Yours Till Banana Splits,* a collection of autograph rhymes; and *Six Sick Sheep,* tongue twisters. We've also compiled anthologies of stories, poems, and jokes, such as: *The Read-Aloud Treasury, The Scary Book, Give a Dog a Bone,* and *Ready… Set…Read!*

Stephanie and my latest writing project together is the *Gator Girls* series, short, humorous novels about two best-friend alligator characters named Allie Gator and Amy Gator. They live in apartment houses next door to each other, and when they aren't together, they're always on the phone. Stephanie and I are like the

Gators: when we're not together, we're talking on the phone, and when we're not on the phone, we're faxing each other. We do a lot of joint writing by phone or fax, but for the *Gator Girls* books, we visit each other to write. Stephanie sits at the computer and types, and I sit behind her, reading what comes up on the screen. We both talk and some combination of what we say gets into the book. Stephanie and I didn't know each other when we were kids, so we couldn't be best friends then like Allie and Amy, but we are the closest of friends now, so we dedicated the first *Gator Girls* book to each other.

Illustrations by Lynn Munsinger from the first book in the Gator Girls *series.*

Once or twice, my husband, Phil, and I have written picture books together. We wrote *Big Goof and Little Goof* while we were driving in the car. Phil was behind the wheel and I was sitting beside him with a pencil and paper. We thought of one short story about two goofy guys who get all mixed up and think that a turtle is a dog. Then we wrote two other stories about the same guys. The three stories went together in one picture book with goofy illustrations by M. K. Brown.

Phil and I aren't quite as goofy as the Goofs, but we do get mixed up sometimes. Once we put an electric blanket on our bed *upside down*. That meant that when I turned the knob on *my* side of the bed, it operated *Phil's* side of the blanket, and he was operating my side, but we didn't know it. I was cold, and kept turning up the blanket. I went from number 2, to number 3 and 4. Finally, I said, "I'm freezing! I'm turning this thing all the way up to 6!" A few minutes later, I was still cold, but Phil jumped out of bed. He'd never been so hot in his life!

Phil and I

Big Goof and Little Goof, illustrated by M. K. Brown.

When I was asked by a publisher to write the book you are reading right now, I felt I needed help to write about myself. So I worked with Wendy Saul, a poet, a college professor, and an expert on science education. Wendy and I sat together in my office. This time, I was at the computer and she was on the other side of my big table with a pile of my books to look at and about a hundred pages of transcripts of interviews she had conducted with me earlier.

I typed, reading aloud as I went. I might be writing about my father mixing paint in the basement, and I might start feeling unsure of myself and say, "Does anyone care about this?" and Wendy would say, "Don't stop. This is good." Sometimes I would start a sentence, and she would finish it. When we got to the chapter on how I write about science, Wendy said, "Try to talk to kids about their own writing" and "Tell how important it is to feel a connection to what you're writing about." I know a lot of things about my work, but sometimes I don't *know* I know them. Wendy helped draw them out.

SEVEN

Is It Fun to Be an Author?

BEING INSIDE THE WRITING

Illustration by Bruce Degen from The Magic School Bus Inside a Hurricane.

Is it fun for me to be a published author? You bet! I get reviews, fan mail, money, and I get to hold the finished books in my hands. I can give them to my mother and my grand-nieces and nephews as presents. I feel proud of what I've accomplished.

But being published, being successful at it, getting awards and attention from others—as terrific as these things are—are not truly what being a writer is about. These are rewards that come from outside me. The *act of writing* is why I write. There is nothing so wonderful as being in the middle of writing something, and it's moving along in a plodding, predictable way, when suddenly everything starts going faster. The paper, the pencil, the computer—all of these seem to disappear, and I become lost in the process. It reminds of a favorite poem by David McCord:

Blesséd Lord, what it is to be young:

To be of, to be for, be among—

Be enchanted, enthralled,

Be the caller, the called,

The singer, the song, and the sung.

Most writers will tell you of similar experiences. And not only writers. This happens to artists, athletes, mechanics, cooks, scientists. It happens to all people who find satisfaction in their work. It happens often to children when they play. I remember having this feeling when I was digging a system of tunnels in my backyard as a child. My mother said it was time for bed, and it was like pulling myself out of a compelling dream. It seemed almost impossible to let go. But then in the morning, there was a delicious sense of anticipation, of such happiness, because I knew I would get back to the feeling as soon as I started digging again. For me, this is an ordinary part of being a writer, and every time it happens, it's extraordinary.

Credits

p.ii, iii, 46, 47—Illustrations from *The Gator Girls* by Joanna Cole and Stephanie Calmenson. Illustrated by Lynn Munsinger. Copyright © 1995 by Lynn Munsinger. By permission of Morrow Junior Books, a division of William Morrow and Company, Inc.

p.3, 12, 29, 31, 35—Illustrations by Bruce Degen from *The Magic School Bus Inside the Human Body* by Joanna Cole. Illustrations copyright © 1989 by Bruce Degen. Reprinted by permission of Scholastic Inc. *The Magic School Bus* is a registered trademark of Scholastic Inc.

p.4—Illustration from *Cockroaches* by Joanna Cole. Illustrated by Jean Zallinger. Copyright © 1971 by Jean Zallinger. By permission of Morrow Junior Books, a division of William Morrow and Company, Inc.

p.5—Illustration by Jared Lee from *Monster Manners* by Joanna Cole. Illustrations copyright © 1985 by Jared Lee. Reprinted by permission of Scholastic Inc.

p.7—Illustration from *Norma Jean, Jumping Bean* by Joanna Cole, illustrated by Lynn Munsinger. Illustrations copyright © 1987 by Lynn Munsinger. Reprinted by permission of Random House, Inc.

p.8—Photograph from *A Frog's Body* by Joanna Cole. Photographs by Jerome Wexler. Photographs copyright © 1980 by Jerome Wexler. By permission of Morrow Junior Books, a division of William Morrow and Company, Inc.

p.9—Cover illustration from *How I Was Adopted* by Joanna Cole. Illustrated by Maxine Chambliss. Illustration copyright © 1995 by Maxine Chambliss. By permission of Morrow Junior Books, a division of William Morrow and Company, Inc.